Bob Mann's
PROVEN
GOLF
METHOD

PUBLICATIONS INTERNATIONAL, LTD.

CONTENTS

Louis Weber
Publications International, Ltd.
7373 North Cicero Avenue
Lincolnwood, Illinois 60646

Permission is never granted for commercial purposes.

Manufactured in Yugoslavia.

h g f e d c b a

ISBN 0-88176-598-8

Author: Bob Mann, creator of the Automatic Golf Method

Photography: Tim DeFrisco/ALLSPORT

Photographed at the Desert Mountain Resort, Carefree, Arizona.

NOTE: Neither Publications International, Ltd., nor the writers or publisher take responsibility for any possible consequences from any program, procedure, or action by any person reading or following the information in this book.

INTRODUCTION

It's 10:24 A.M. A crowd of people has gathered in a field behind the runway of a small airport. At 10:30, the biplane, now taxiing down the runway, is scheduled for takeoff. Inside the plane, the new pilot, seated in the cockpit, meticulously rechecks the instrument panel as he awaits final clearance from the tower. As his signal comes in, he revs up the engine. The plane begins to accelerate, rolling down the runway, picking up speed with every passing second. Then, it happens. The plane is lifted into the air in a dynamic, seemingly effortless motion.

"He did it!" someone shouts from below. "Wow, did you see that takeoff? Wasn't that incredible?"

Incredible as it may seem to spectators, the success of this takeoff is simply the product of precise preflight preparation. When this preparation is carried through, the magnificent takeoff is something that *just happens*.

Why am I talking about airplanes and takeoffs in a book about golf? For one very important reason! A successful golf swing, like a successful takeoff, is merely the product of the proper preparation. When the preparation is there, the swing *just happens*.

That's what this book is all about—PRE-SWING PREPARATION—how to do it right from the very beginning. Hundreds of thousands of golfers have used my method to produce a powerful and accurate golf swing—and YOU CAN, TOO. No matter who you are, my method will help you develop a swing that will work for you—a swing that you can depend on time and time again. And it'll work because it's based on PROVEN BIOMECHANICAL PRINCIPLES that relate *not only* to golf but to a variety of *other* physical activities. These principles produce the power and accuracy you are seeking in your golf swing.

Your study of this book will give you a basic understanding of my method. To enjoy the benefits, however, YOU MUST APPLY these principles and PRACTICE your golf motor move as I've explained it—because in the final analysis, golf is a physical event, not an intellectual one. My advice then? Don't just think about it. DO IT!

And maybe one day, after you've teed off, you'll hear someone in your crowd say, "Wow! Did you see that swing? Wasn't *that* incredible?"

Pre-swing preparation produces controlled backswing.

Controlled backswing produces birdies.

THE GRIP

Your grip sets the tone for your entire golf swing. If the pressure points you establish are inadequate or misplaced, your swing will be inhibited and ineffective no matter what else you do correctly. Conversely, if you've got the proper grip, there's very little that can happen to interfere with a good swing and ultimately a good shot.

The following instructions apply to right-handed players. For LEFT-HANDED PLAYERS, simply reverse directions.

TO PREPARE FOR THE PROPER GRIP:

Hold the club in your right hand with the right arm fully extended at about chest height. Notice the angle between the arm and the club. Also note the point of contact—on the shaft just below the club's grip.

DO NOT GRIP THE CLUB WHILE IT'S RESTING ON THE TURF.

Note angle between arm and club.

◀ Proper grip: golfer's view

LEFT HAND

1. Hold your left hand out in front of you. Rotate the hand until the KNUCKLES of the forefinger and middle finger are the ONLY ones that are clearly visible.

2. Imagine that a straight line exists down the length of your lower arm through the thumb of your left hand. Turn your thumb slightly to the LEFT OF THIS MIDLINE until it just about touches the inside surface of the first joint of the forefinger. In other words, there's no space between the thumb and the pad of the hand.

3. Form a hook with the left forefinger, bringing its fingertip almost in contact with the pad of the thumb (the portion of the thumb that you would use to produce a thumbprint).

4. In this position, close the hand as though you were SQUEEZING A SMALL LEMON with ONLY THE LAST THREE FINGERS, bringing the tips of these fingers in contact with the hand, just to the right of the fleshy pad at the base of the thumb.

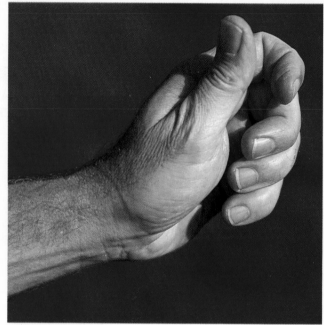

Proper "preformed" left hand

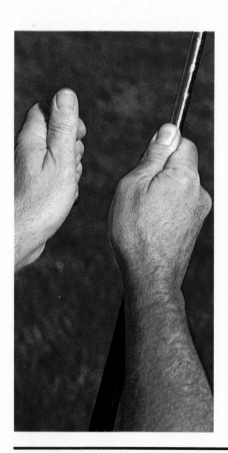

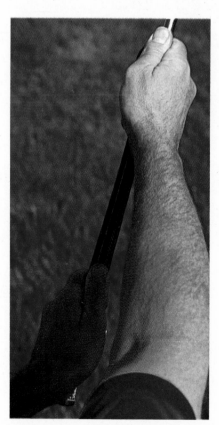

5. While maintaining this position, open the hand slightly. Then, SLIDE the hand into a position on the club that allows approximately ½ inch of club to extend out beyond the lowermost portion of the hand. Make certain that the bottom edge of the club is aligned parallel to the midline of your body and therefore at a right angle to the intended line of the ball's flight. In golf vernacular, the *clubface is square.*

THE CLUB SHOULD NOW BE FULLY EXTENDED IN FRONT OF YOU.

**Left: Open preformed hand slightly.
Right: Slide hand into position on club.**

IF YOU ARE GRIPPING THE CLUB CORRECTLY WITH YOUR LEFT HAND, YOU WILL NOTICE THAT:

1. The original angle that you established between your club and your arm will be maintained.

2. Your gripping pressure will be focused in your last three fingers.

Locate tendons and check alignment.

3. The space between the tendons at the inner side surface of your wrist will be lined up with the shaft of your club.

4. Your left thumb will take on a "short" position on the shaft. In other words, your thumb will be pulled toward you, so that only the pad that would be used to produce a thumbprint is pressed against the club. The left forefinger, as a result, will take on a "long" position.

5. The club will not flop if you relax your thumb and forefinger.

The following examples are two common *LEFT-HAND GRIP ERRORS.*

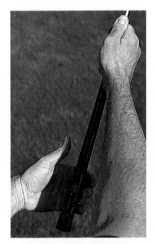 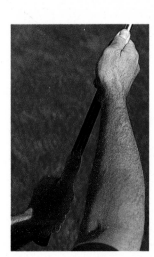

Left: incorrect wrapping of hand
Right: incorrect "long" thumb position

1. In attempting to achieve the proper grip, many beginning golfers WRAP the left hand around the club rather than SLIDING the hand into place already "preformed." This technique causes the finger and hand alignment to vary from grip to grip and fails to emphasize the proper pressure points.

2. Some beginning golfers may also use the "LONG" thumb approach to gripping the club, in which the left thumb extends too far down the shaft. This prevents the last three fingers from exerting maximum pressure on the club.

LEFT-HAND REVIEW

1. ROTATE. (KNUCKLES) Rotate the hand until the first and second knuckles are the ONLY ones clearly visible.

2. TURN. (THUMB) Turn your thumb to the left of the midline.

3. HOOK. (FOREFINGER) Form a hook with your forefinger, bringing the fingertip pad almost in contact with the last pad of your thumb.

4. SQUEEZE. Close your hand as though you were about to squeeze a small lemon with the last three fingers of your hand.

5. SLIDE. Slide the preformed hand into proper position on the club.

IF YOU ARE GRIPPING THE CLUB CORRECTLY WITH YOUR LEFT HAND:

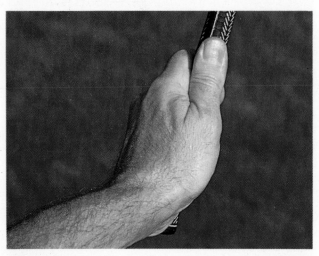

Correct left-hand grip

1. The appropriate angle will be established between the club and your arm.

2. Your gripping pressure will be concentrated in your last three fingers.

3. The space between the tendons at the inner surface of your wrist will be in line with the shaft of your club.

4. Your left thumb will be in the "short" position.

5. Your club will not flop if you relax your thumb and forefinger.

IF YOU ARE NOT GRIPPING THE CLUB CORRECTLY, START THE GRIPPING PROCESS ALL OVER AGAIN FROM THE BEGINNING. DON'T TRY TO MAKE ADJUSTMENTS ONCE THE PROCESS HAS BEGUN.

When you have assumed the proper left-hand grip, LET GO OF THE CLUB WITH THE RIGHT HAND while maintaining the club in its position in front of you at about chest height with your left arm fully extended. Now you're ready to grip the club with your right hand.

The right hand has ONLY ONE ROLE in relationship to your swing. That role is to STABILIZE your club through impact with the ball.

RIGHT HAND

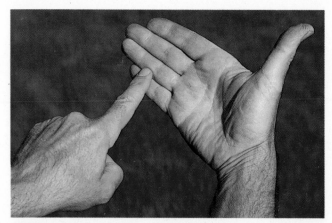

Middle pads

1. Locate the MIDDLE PADS on the inside surface of the middle and ring fingers.

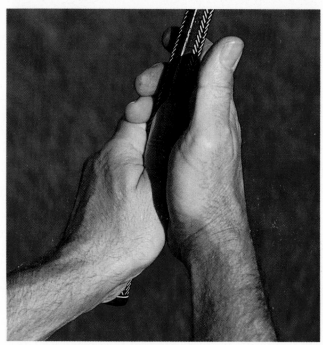

Correct placement of middle pads

2. Place these pads DIRECTLY UNDER your club as you slide your ring finger against the forefinger of the left hand.

3. Slip the PINKY of your right hand into the space between the forefinger and middle finger of the left hand.

4. Close the middle and ring fingers of the right hand around the club.

5. With the right thumb now turned to the left, create a pocket between the right thumb and the rest of the hand. Then, relax the pocket down over the left thumb. This pocket or crease should fit comfortably over the left thumb without squeezing or exerting pressure. This left-thumb/right-hand-pocket relationship establishes a perfect blending of the two hands into a single, unified grip.

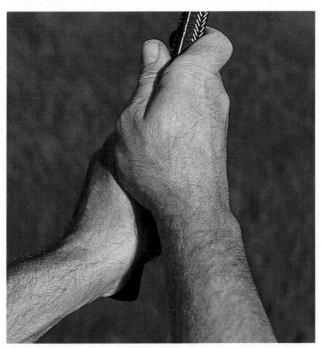

Note hook-shaped forefinger and relaxed thumb.

6. Allow your right forefinger to form a RESTING hook-shaped support behind the club.

IF YOU ARE GRIPPING THE CLUB CORRECTLY WITH YOUR RIGHT HAND, YOU WILL NOTICE THAT:

1. The pinky of the right hand will slip NATURALLY into the space between the forefinger and the middle finger of the left hand.

2. The pocket between the right thumb and the rest of the hand will fit NATURALLY over the left thumb.

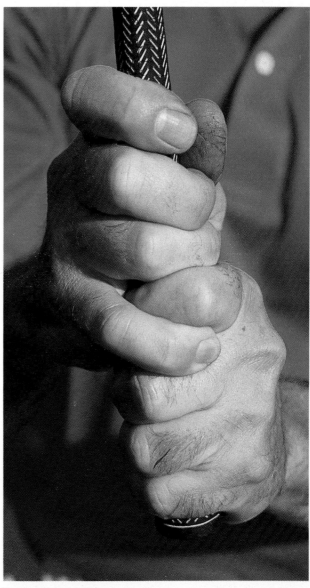

Note position of pinky.

3. The thumb of the right hand will NOT EXERT FORCE on the club.

4. The only pressure exerted on the club by the right hand will come from the middle and ring fingers with a slight pressure in the crook of the right forefinger that is created by the correct placement and squeezing action of the two fingers directly below it.

The following examples are two common *RIGHT-HAND GRIP ERRORS.*

Left: incorrect position of club in crease
Right: incorrect thumb and forefinger
position

1. Oftentimes an error occurs when the beginning golfer allows the club to roll into the crease at the base of the fingers. This maneuver activates improper muscles that inhibit your swing.

2. Another common mistake involves the squeezing of the club by the right forefinger and thumb, which also inhibits the free dynamic action of the swing. Remember, the ONLY role of the right hand is to STABILIZE the club through impact.

RIGHT-HAND REVIEW

1. PADS. Find the middle pads of the middle and ring fingers.

2. SLIDE. Place these pads under your club and slide your ring finger over the forefinger of the left hand.

3. PINKY. Slip the pinky into the space between the forefinger and middle finger of the left hand.

4. CLOSE. Close the middle and ring fingers of the right hand around the club.

5. THUMB. Create a pocket between the right thumb and the rest of the hand. Then, relax the pocket down over the left thumb.

6. FOREFINGER. Allow your right forefinger to form an inactive "hooked" support behind the club.

Note right-hand "short" thumb position
in proper grip.

Proper grip: right-side view

IF YOU ARE GRIPPING THE CLUB CORRECTLY WITH YOUR RIGHT HAND:

1. The pinky of your right hand will fit comfortably into the space between your left forefinger and middle finger.

2. The pocket between your right thumb and the rest of your hand will fit comfortably over your left thumb.

3. The right thumb will exert no force on the club.

4. The only force exerted on the club by the right hand will come from the middle and ring fingers with only slight pressure in the crook of the right forefinger created by the correct placement and squeezing action of the two fingers directly below it.

AS BEFORE, IF YOU ARE GRIPPING THE CLUB INCORRECTLY WITH YOUR RIGHT HAND, START THE RIGHT-HAND PLACEMENT AGAIN.

Practice these GRIP INSTRUCTIONS until the entire process becomes quick, comfortable, and AUTOMATIC. Your investment of time now will pay off greatly later with terrific swings and solid shots.

LOWERING THE CLUB

If you have established the proper grip, your hands and arms will be in a NEUTRAL POSITION. By neutral position, I mean that your clubface is square—its lower edge is at a right angle to the intended line of flight—and the relationship between the club and your arms is the same as it will be throughout the backswing. As you lower the club, it's important to maintain this neutral position.

Note angle between arms and club.

TO PROPERLY LOWER THE CLUB:

1. Maintain a relaxed but erect posture.

◄ Proper swing muscles in command

Feet spread apart to about shoulder width

2. Spread your feet about as far apart as the width of your shoulders. This will vary depending upon which club you are using. (I will explain this further in the chapter on club positions.)

3. Turn your left foot slightly out to the left.

LOWERING THE CLUB

16

4. Lower the club by lowering your arms from the shoulders. DO NOT BEND FROM THE WAIST.

5. Keep your head erect, aligned with your spine. DO NOT LOWER YOUR HEAD.

6. MAINTAIN THE PREESTABLISHED ANGLE BETWEEN YOUR ARMS AND YOUR CLUB.

Lower club from shoulders without bending over.

7. As the clubhead reaches the approximate level of your knees, start "SITTING DOWN"—flex your knees and shift your weight to your heels, thus bringing the clubhead to just above contact with the turf.

Note right thumb on left side of shaft.

Inset: incorrect grounding of club on turf
Correct: club held off contact with turf

8. Turn your chin slightly to the right so that you'll be viewing the back of the ball with your left eye.

Inset: chin-to-right position
Note erect head.

Note how back of ball is viewed through left eye.

LOWERING-OF-THE-CLUB ERRORS

1. Bending from the waist may seem like an easy way to lower your golf club...but it's the wrong way! When you bend from the waist, you'll probably end up locking your knees—a position that eliminates any chance of achieving the proper swing motion. The majority of novice golfers will attempt a golf swing with their knees locked, their weight shifted to the balls of their feet, and a straight-line extension between their arms and their golf clubs. IT IS VIRTUALLY IMPOSSIBLE TO EXECUTE A PROPER GOLF SWING ONCE THIS INCORRECT POSITION HAS BEEN ASSUMED.

2. Many beginning golfers will LOWER THEIR HEADS as they lower their golf clubs. Bending the head down creates undesirable tension between the shoulder blades. Moreover, it results in the inability of the right shoulder to rotate past the chin through the impact zone. Solid contact and on-line flight require that the shoulders rotate through the shot without the head turning until *well after impact*. It is therefore necessary that you maintain a head-up position throughout the swing—so that the shoulder turn is not blocked by the head.

Those who lower their heads during swing preparation also have the tendency to lock their knees. The knees must remain flexed to permit the dynamic leg motion that creates accurate and powerful shots. So remember... head up, knees flexed.

Incorrect: knees locked and arm/club angle not maintained

Incorrect: Head-down position cramps
swing.

THE GOLF MOTOR EXERCISE

Recall proper starting position. For golf motor exercise, use only left hand.

You've now learned the right grip and body position to initiate an efficient, consistent golf swing. But, you're probably not quite ready to produce the swing itself. Before you can complete a swing that is both powerful and on target, you need to activate what I call your "golf motor"—the power source of your feet and legs. Once you learn to activate this motor, you'll be able to set in motion a *dynamic, accurate, and powerful swing each* and every time you pick up your club. With practice, you'll gradually experience the beautiful rhythm of a correct swing—a rhythm that you won't forget. Your swing will become truly AUTOMATIC.

THE MOTOR EXERCISE

The following exercise will involve gripping the club with the LEFT HAND ONLY. (Note: With the exception of this one-handed placement, the first portion of this exercise reviews the proper technique for lowering your club.)

1. Assume the proper placement of your left hand on the club.

2. Maintain a relaxed but erect posture with your feet apart to about shoulder width and your left foot pointed slightly out to the left.

◀ **Full extension with club under control during golf motor exercise**

3. Begin to lower your club from your shoulders, keeping your head properly aligned with your spine. Remember, DO NOT BEND FROM YOUR WAIST and DO NOT LOWER YOUR HEAD.

4. MAINTAIN THE PREESTABLISHED ANGLE BETWEEN YOUR ARM AND YOUR CLUB.

5. When your clubhead is lowered to about the level of your knees, SIT DOWN—flex your knees and shift your weight to the heels of your feet, thus bringing the clubhead to just above contact with the turf.

DO NOT LOWER THE CLUB to the turf by STRAIGHTENING YOUR WRIST and casting the clubhead down. IT IS ESSENTIAL THAT THE ANGLE between your arm and your club BE MAINTAINED. This CAN ONLY BE ACHIEVED if the FINAL LOWERING of the club RESULTS FROM FLEXING YOUR KNEES (sitting down into the starting position).

6. Turn your chin slightly to the right so that you'll be viewing the back of the ball with your left eye.

NOW YOU'RE READY TO START YOUR GOLF MOTOR.

Right hand hangs freely during motor exercise.

Proper starting position for motor exercise

7. Roll your right foot to the left—an action that slightly raises your right heel off the ground and shifts your weight to the left. As a result of this action, ALLOW your hand and club TO BE MOVED slightly to your left so that your body is now partially coiled.

Motion begins with right foot.

Right heel slightly raised off ground

Body coiled slightly to left

8. Now roll your left foot to the right—an action that slightly raises your left heel off the ground and shifts your weight to the right. As a result of this action, ALLOW your hand and club TO BE MOVED to your right.

9. Roll your feet from side to side making the motion continuous, drawing more and more power from your legs, while ALLOWING YOUR CLUB to swing more fully each time.

Note left knee as backswing begins.

Left knee moves right.

Top of backswing

Downswing begins with movement of lower body.

Angle between arm and club increases during downswing.

Both knees flexed just before impact

Centrifugal force causes arm and shaft
to be aligned and shaft to be energized.

Chin pointed right, long after impact
zone passed

Chin still back

High finish

There is NO ONE PROPER SWING LENGTH that applies to all golfers. As you continue to roll your feet from side to side, the swing, on its own, will become longer and longer until it becomes YOUR full swing. The length of your swing, therefore, will be controlled by your physical makeup and flexibility.

IF YOU ARE DOING THE MOTOR EXERCISE CORRECTLY, YOU WILL NOTICE THAT:

1. All of the movement you experience will be INITIATED ONLY BY YOUR FEET AND LEGS. Your upper body and club will be MERELY RESPONDING to this rhythmic motion.

2. Your hand, arm, or shoulders will NOT be responsible for the movement of your club.

3. As you ALLOW THE CLUB TO RESPOND TO the movement initiated by your feet and legs, your club will move effortlessly through the air, creating an unmistakably clear and recognizable sound—the sound of a golf swing. If you have to ask if the sound you're hearing is correct—it probably isn't! Once you've produced the proper swing, you'll recognize it immediately.

Remember this: Any moving of the club BY your hand, arm, or shoulders is COUNTERPRODUCTIVE and will only serve to inhibit the true potential of your swing. Your upper body should merely RESPOND TO the movement initiated by your feet and legs.

Practice this exercise until you can swing the club about 15 times consecutively with each swing being of approximately equal rhythm, power, and sound, AND WITHOUT the occurrence of wrist flopping. For the average golfer, this will take about ten to 14 days. The beginning golfer may require a week or two longer to develop a good golf motor move. Periodic rest days during this time will speed up your rate of progress.

DOUBLE YOUR POWER

It's important to note two mechanical aspects of your golf swing. One involves your swing *axis*, and the other involves your swing *lever*.

In the PROPER swing, your club's movement rotates about an axis—that axis being your left shoulder. The lever of this movement includes both your left arm AND the entire shaft of your club.

In the IMPROPER swing, your club's movement also rotates about an axis—but the axis is your wrists, and therefore the lever of this movement consists ONLY of the length of your golf club.

Thus, you can see that the proper swing has almost TWICE the leverage or mechanical advantage as does the improper swing because the lever length—consisting of BOTH the arm and the club—is almost twice as long.

AXIS

LEVER

Proper swing has mechanical advantage.

THE SWING

When the golf motor exercise feels comfortable and easy, when you can swing the club as steady and sure the fifteenth time as you did the first, when the balance and rhythm of the swing feel like second nature to you, AND when wrist flopping does not occur, THEN—and ONLY THEN—are you ready to attempt a full golf swing using BOTH hands.

It's important to note that the addition of your right hand MUST NOT add to, or take away from, the natural, rhythmic motion of the swing that you've developed by practicing the motor move while gripping the club with only your left hand. Remember, the only role of the right hand is to help STABILIZE your club through impact with the ball. It should NOT be used to influence the force or direction of your swing.

To familiarize yourself with the moves and "looks" of a properly executed swing, the pages in this section will follow the swing sequence from beginning to end, step by step, frame by frame. Observe the sequence carefully so that you will be getting a strong visual reinforcement of the proper swinging motion. It's important to keep in mind, however, that you CANNOT ACHIEVE the proper swing by looking at it and analyzing it. The proper swing is something you CAN ONLY ACHIEVE as a PRODUCT OF the proper grip, body position, starter move, and motor exercise.

Motor exercise helps swing development.

◀ Dynamite finish

33

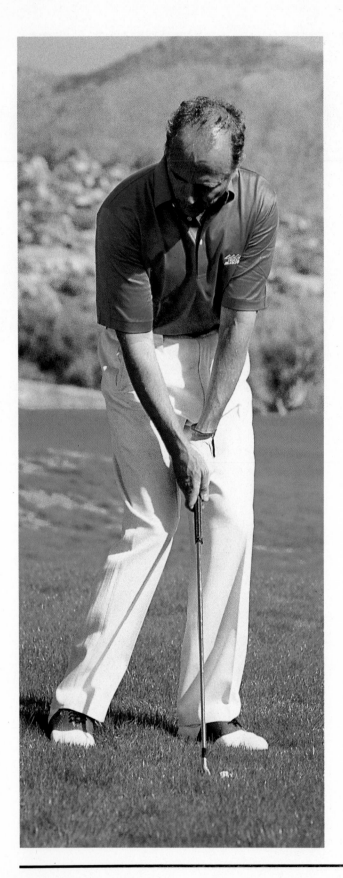

Golf swing starts with rolling action of right foot.

THE STARTER MOVE

The motion of the golf swing starts with the feet and legs. Notice how I activate my golf motor by rolling my right foot to the left—an action that slightly raises my right heel off the turf and shifts my weight to the left.

As a result of this action, I allow my hands and club to be moved to the left so that my body is now partially coiled.

THE BACKSWING BEGINS

The backswing begins with the
left foot as I roll it to the right—
an action that raises my left heel
off the turf and shifts my weight
to the right.

The motion of my lower body
propels my upper body and
ultimately my club to the peak of
the backswing.

Notice that the preestablished
relationship between my arms
and club has not changed.

Note also that my chin is pointed
to the right.

Backswing starts with left foot.

Left heel rolls off turf.

**Preestablished angle between arms and
club is maintained during backswing.**

Angle between arm and club remains the same.

THE TOP OF THE SWING

Although this is technically the top of the backswing, my club will continue to move farther back as my lower body reverses directions to begin the downswing.

Left knee begins move toward target.

THE DOWNSWING BEGINS

Herein lies the unique feature of the properly executed downswing. As my lower body begins the downswing, my upper body is STILL MOVING BACK. As a result of this action, my lower body will return to the impact zone BEFORE my upper body and club.

The ANGLE between my arms and club has now INCREASED as a result of the centrifugal force created by the movement of my lower body. This shifting of my weight to the left, as led by the lower part of my body, pulls my club toward a more inside path— one that's *inside* the path of the backswing.

THE POWER SOURCE

The shaft of my club is now energized. As my lower body moves back in the direction of the target, a pulling force is exerted on my upper body causing my arms, hands, and clubhead to return to the ball. This delay between the return of the lower and upper parts of my body will ultimately increase the power of my swing.

IMPACT

My chin is maintained in its starting position, pointed behind the ball.

My body has taken on a C-like position with my hips moved to the left and my head and feet moved to the right.

My club's path of attack on the downswing is inside the path of the backswing. Remember, this change of path occurs automatically as a result of the movement of my upper body—a movement that is RESPONSIVE to the movement of the lower body, not INITIATED by the upper body itself. After assuming the proper grip and starting position, my entire golf swing is as simple as this: MY LOWER BODY INITIATES THE DOWNSWING. EVERYTHING THAT MY UPPER BODY AND CLUB NEED TO DO WILL OCCUR WITHOUT THOUGHT OR EFFORT IN RESPONSE TO THE MOVEMENT OF MY LOWER BODY.

Chin back; knees flexed; great shot!

THE FINISH

My weight is shifted to the outside of my left foot.

My chin is no longer pointed behind the ball. The force of my swing has brought my shoulders and head through the shot AFTER impact. No conscious effort on my part has been made to cause this movement of my head. To the contrary, there is a conscious effort to HOLD MY CHIN BACK as long as possible.

The desirable high finish occurs automatically as a product of the proper preceding move.

Lower body has moved to left.

Swing produced by lower body creates
high finish.

Centrifugal force completes swing.

Head has turned toward target long after impact.

Knees pointed toward target

Completion of automatic swing

Relaxed high finish

CLUB POSITIONS

Well, you've read about it; you've seen pictures of what it looks like. Now, it's your turn to do it. A properly executed swing is within your power. Just remember this: With the proper setup, a successful swing will occur virtually automatically.

So, how do you begin? The procedure for assuming the proper starting position will be the same for all clubs except the putter. To assume this position, spread your feet apart to approximately shoulder width and align your toes with an imaginary line that runs parallel to the intended line of flight. The relationship of your clubhead to your left foot will be the same for all clubs. That position is approximately two inches to the right of the left heel. The width of your stance and the position of your RIGHT foot will vary depending upon the length of your club.

The appropriate stance and right-foot adjustments are described on the following pages.

Proper setup produces a swing like this when proper position is assumed.

◀ Correct positioning of feet will effect outcome of shot.

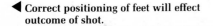

DRIVER

The driver is the longest club in the golf bag. The objective in swinging the driver is to produce the fullest possible controlled backswing so as to maximize the distance the ball will travel.

To accomplish this, two adjustments are necessary:

• The first involves adopting a STANCE SLIGHTLY WIDER THAN SHOULDER WIDTH. The widening of your stance gives you a more stable base for controlling the greater forces imposed by the longer shaft of the driver.

• The second involves WITHDRAWING THE RIGHT FOOT about two inches from the intended line of flight. In golf vernacular, this is referred to as a CLOSED STANCE. Closing the stance enables you to make a freer turn AWAY from the ball during your backswing—an action that enhances BOTH power and distance.

The closed stance will enable you to produce a longer, more desirable backswing. The wider stance will provide you with the greater stability necessary to control it.

With slight modifications to a less wide and less closed stance, your position will be the same for the fairway woods and the long irons as it is for the driver.

Widen your stance for longer clubs.
Inset: Withdraw right foot about two inches from line of flight.

MIDDLE IRONS

No alteration of your right-foot position is required for the proper execution of the middle-iron shots. In other words, you will maintain your stance with your feet spread apart to approximately shoulder width. This position is refered to as a SQUARE STANCE.

Use shoulder-width stance for middle irons.

SHORT IRONS

The objective of the short-iron shot is quite the opposite from the driver. The objective in swinging the short iron is to produce a more accurate shot.

To hit a successful short-iron shot, two adjustments are necessary:

• The first involves PUSHING THE RIGHT FOOT FORWARD *across* the intended line of flight. In golf vernacular, this is referred to as an OPEN STANCE. Opening the stance restricts your turn during your backswing—an action that enhances accuracy at the expense of distance.

• The second involves adopting a STANCE SLIGHTLY NAR-ROWER THAN SHOULDER WIDTH. Since you're using a shorter club and, as the result of the open stance, will be experiencing a more restricted backswing, a narrower base is adequate to maintain stability.

The open stance will enable you to produce a more accurate shot by restricting your backswing. The narrowed stance will provide you with stability sufficient for this restricted movement.

Narrow your stance for shorter clubs. Push right foot forward across line of flight.

STANCE ADJUSTMENTS IN SUMMARY

The longer the club, the wider and more closed the stance. The shorter the club, the narrower and more open the stance. A bit of experimentation on your part will enable you to establish your best right-foot position for each of the shots. Although every golfer must fine-tune his or her own stance, the principles stated above are constant.

Good setup including proper stance produces great swings.

METHOD SUMMARY

Well, the book that started out about airplanes and takeoffs is about to come in for a landing! I began this book by telling you that a successful golf swing, like a successful takeoff, is merely the product of the proper preparation.

To that end, I've provided you with an easy, step-by-step presentation of my golf method. Once you've mastered the techniques I've outlined, that successful swing and solid shot you've always

hoped for will happen automatically—just like that magnificent takeoff—in one dynamic, seemingly effortless motion…time and time again.

What follows is an overview of the most important steps to remember—steps that encompass the biomechanical principles that make my method work. Subscribe to these principles as I do, and your rewards will be unparalled.

KEY POINTS IN REVIEW

1. Hold your club in your right hand with the right arm fully extended at about chest height.

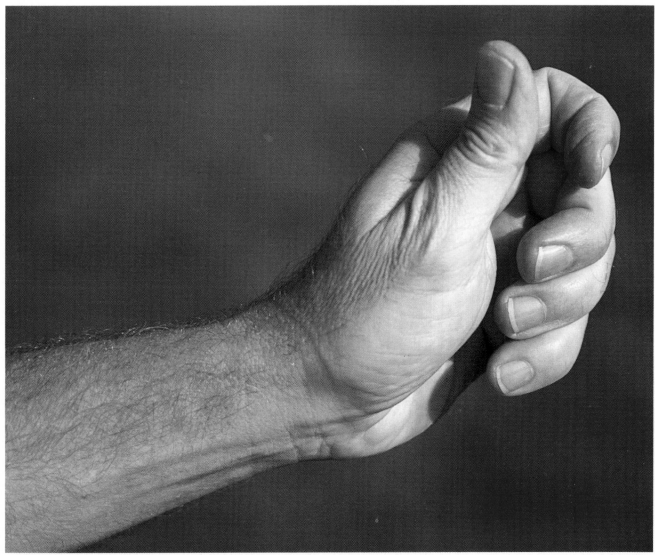

2. Preform the left hand into a "short" thumb position.

3. Slide your left hand into place on the club.

METHOD SUMMARY

4. Concentrate your gripping pressure largely in the last three fingers of your left hand. Let go with the right hand while being certain to maintain the preestablished angle between your arm and your club.

5. Check the alignment of your left hand by locating the space between the two tendons at the outside base of the thumb. Be certain that the space is in line with the shaft of your club.

6. Grip the club lightly with the middle two fingers of the right hand. (Remember, the right hand is used *ONLY* to stabilize your club through impact.) Do not exert any squeezing pressure on your club with your right thumb and forefinger.

7. Use a wider and more closed stance when you select a longer club.

8. Use a narrower and more open stance when you select a shorter club.

9. Lower your club by lowering your arms from the shoulders. Do not bend at the waist.

10. Keep your head erect, aligned with your spine. Do not bend your head down.

11. As your clubhead reaches the approximate level of your knees, flex your knees and shift your weight to your heels. Bring your clubhead to just above contact with the turf.

12. Turn your chin to the right so that you'll be viewing the back of the ball with your left eye.

13. Activate your golf motor by rolling your right foot to the left—an action that raises your right heel off the turf and shifts your weight to the left.

14. Initiate your backswing by rolling your left foot to the right—an action that raises your left heel off the turf and shifts your weight to the right.

15. As you complete your backswing, make a conscious effort to keep your chin pointed to the right until well after impact.

With proper preparation and a conscious effort to maintain the chin-to-right position, a great swing *just happens automatically*.